Snowflakes On My Nose

Activity Book

Written by Erin Alladin

Printed in China by Qualibre Inc. / Print Plus

Pajama Press, Inc.
469 Richmond St. E, Toronto, ON M5A 1R1

Distributed in Canada by UTP Distribution
5201 Dufferin Street Toronto, Ontario Canada, M3H 5T8

Distributed in the U.S. by Ingram Publisher Services
1 Ingram Blvd. La Vergne, TN 37086, USA

Let's solve the puzzle!

How many more **mittens** are there than **hats**?
Color the correct number.

Let's color!

word search

SNOW COAT COLD
WINTER SCARF

S	N	O	W	A	B
C	Z	E	I	F	C
H	J	L	N	N	O
C	O	A	T	I	L
M	G	K	E	O	D
S	C	A	R	F	P

Let's color!

Use the code to color each section. A secret picture will be revealed.

GREY - 1   BROWN - 2   BLUE - 3

RED - 4   PINK - 5   BLACK - 6

Complete the poem!

Choose the rhyming word to complete the poem.

LITTLE ROUND SMALL

Take some snow
And roll a ball.
This one's big
And this one's _____!

Let's color!

Let's draw!

Every snowflake has **six equal sides**.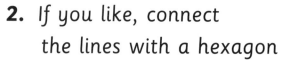

1. Draw three lines
crossed in the middle

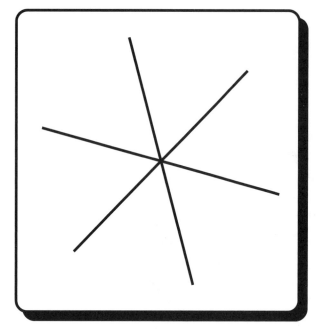

2. If you like, connect
the lines with a hexagon

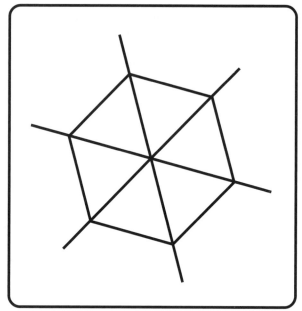

3. Decorate!

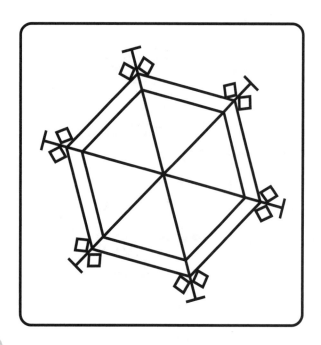

4. Try decorating
some snowflakes!

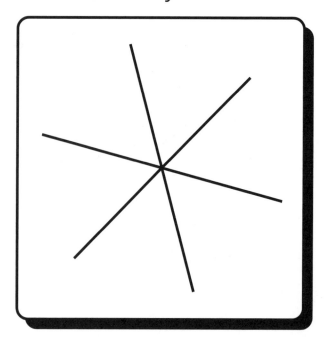

Let's draw!

Draw some **snowflakes** for these kids to catch.

Complete the silly story

Choose each word from the box that matches the line.

One winter, my _____ pet

.... got lost in

a _____ snowdrift. First we

dug ~~~~~~~~~~~~~~~~with our

mittens. Then we dug ~~~~~~~~~~~~~~~

with shovels. It was no good. In the end we had

to dig with a _ _ _ _ _ _ _ _ _ _ _ _ _ _ _ _.

When we finally dug deep enough, there she

was, ~~~~~~~~~~~~~~~ using

a _ _ _ _ _ _ _ _ _ _ _ _ _ _ to build a snow

....

ADJECTIVES

Happy
Goofy
Huge
Pink
Quiet
Scary
Fluffy
Tiny
Useful

ANIMALS

Cat
Dog
Rabbit
Camel
Gerbil
Penguin
Goose
Rat

OBJECTS

Toothbrush
Frying pan
Tractor
Ice-cream scoop
Cookbook
Scissors
Flowerpot
Teacup
Bulldozer

ADVERBS

Happily
Anxiously
Eagerly
Quickly
Sneakily
Angrily
Slowly

Let's solve the puzzle!

Find the path to the chalet where every answer is **5**.

2 + 3

4 + 1

6 - 2

2 + 2

5 - 0

1 + 2

7 - 2

4 - 1

1 + 4

CHALET

Let's solve the puzzle!

Join the dots.

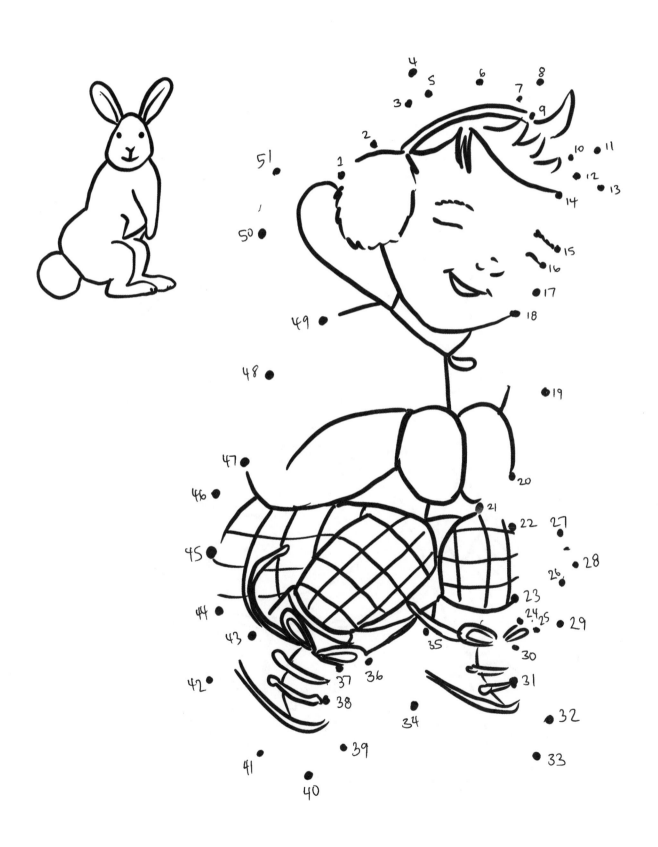

Let's solve the puzzle!

Find these shapes in the picture.

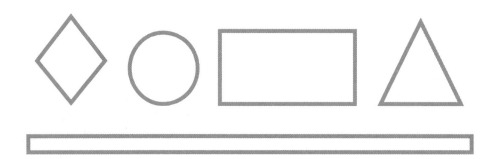

Snowflakes on My Nose

Let's solve the puzzle!

Roll the **snowball** all the way to the **snowman**.

Let's match!

Match each animal to its shadow.

Scavenger Hunt

Can you spot these things the next time you are out in the snow?

- ☐ Animal tracks

- ☐ Boot prints with an interesting pattern

- ☐ A lost hat, mitten, or scarf

- ☐ A snowman or snow fort

- ☐ A leaf still attached to a branch

- ☐ Icicles

Let's solve the puzzle!

Which **bird** made these tracks?

Let's solve the puzzle!

Which **hat** comes next in the pattern?

Let's draw!

Learn to draw a **spruce tree**.

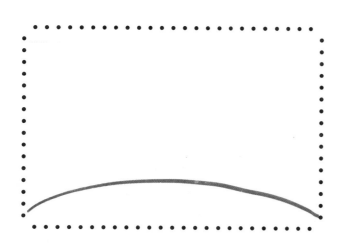

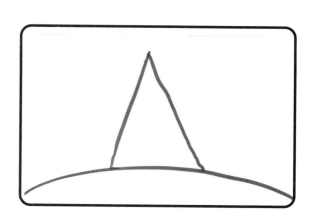

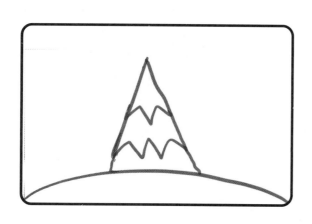

You draw!

Sticky Snow

Packing snow is needed for making snowballs and snowmen.

Fresh snow with perfect six-sided flakes makes the best packing snow.

The **"glue"** that makes it sticky is water.

That's why the best temperatures for packing snow are just above or just below freezing.

Making

Look who has been
walking through the snow!

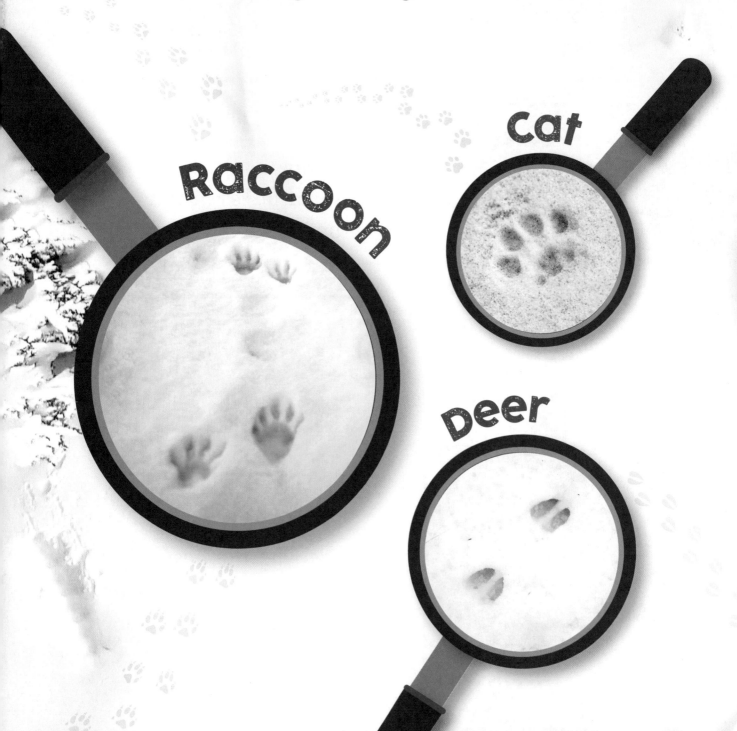

Cat

Raccoon

Deer

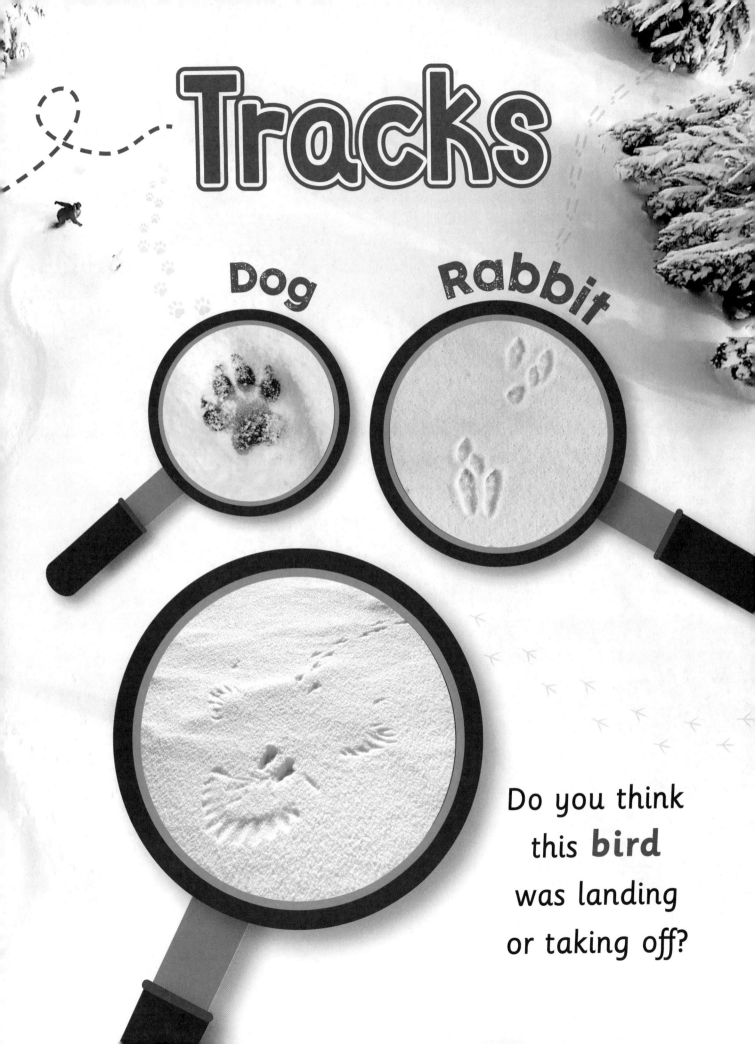

Tracks

Dog

Rabbit

Do you think this **bird** was landing or taking off?

IS IT TRUE
that no two snowflakes are the same?

Scientists say that it probably is true. Some can look similar, but their many crystals have tiny differences.

Snowflakes are made of tiny ice crystals that form around a speck of dust or pollen high in the sky.

Look for yourself! Catch snowflakes on a dark-colored piece of paper to see their crystals up close.

Snowflakes are **symmetrical**. If you folded them down the middle, the two halves would line up perfectly.

Make Your Own
Paper-Collage Snowflakes

1. Cut 3 thin strips of paper

2. Glue your paper strips together in a snowflake shape

3. Fold a piece of paper into 3 layers

4. Cut out shapes (triangles, squares, circles, etc.) through all 3 layers of paper

5. Glue the cut shapes onto the snowflake base from Step 2. For symmetry, use the same pattern of shapes on each strip.

6. Experiment by using different papers. Mix and match the shapes to make a unique snowflake every time.

Making Snow

This is a **fan gun**.

It sprays water through its nozzles in tiny drops.

The drops freeze, and the fan blows them across the hill.

Cold, dry weather is best for making **snow**

for Ski Hills

A **groomer** spreads the snow evenly.

Now the slope
is ready for **skiers!**

Making Maple Syrup

At the end of winter, when days are warm but nights are freezing, **maple sap** is ready to be collected.

A hole is made in a maple tree...

and a **spile** is gently hammered in.

The spile's **spout** drips sap and its **hook** holds the bucket.

The sap is boiled for many hours.

It takes about **40 gallons of sap** to make 1 gallon of syrup!

Which winter sports have you tried?

Downhill Skiing

Sledding

Snowboarding

Ice Skating

Cross-Country Skiing

Tubing

Snowshoeing

Bird Suet Treats

Step 1 Add all ingredients into a big bowl

1 cup
peanut
butter

1 cup melted
suet/lard

sunflower seeds

1/2 cup
cornmeal

unsalted nuts

Mix together

1/2 cup flour

birdseed

Step 2 Press mixture flat
and cut out shapes

cookie cutters

Step 3 Poke hole
with straw
and let dry

Step 4 Tie with
string and
hang in tree

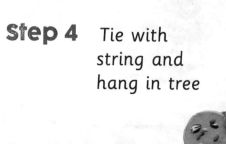

Winter Roosting Pockets (to shelter winter birds)

Step 1

- Crisscross twigs for base
- Tie at center with string
- Begin weaving with twigs, under-over-under-over in circle to make base

willow twigs/dried grasses

natural cotton string

Step 2

- Bring up side twigs and continue weaving over-under-over-under

*leave opening for door hole

Step 3

- Tie string or grasses around top to secure
- Add loop of string to hang on tree

DID YOU KNOW

Much of the art in this activity book comes from these wonderful picture books?

Snow Days
Written by Deborah Kerbel
Illustrated by Miki Sato
ISBN: 9781772781359 (hardcover)
| 9781772782202 (board book)
24 Pages

"*Snow Days* walks through the magic of winter in charming rhyming couplets. Meticulous paper and fabric cutouts form illustrations that seem to leap off of the page..."—**Foreword Reviews**

Birds on Wishbone Street
Written and illustrated by
Suzanne Del Rizzo
ISBN: 9781772782196
(hardcover)
40 Pages

By the creator of the **New York Times** Notable Book **Birds on Wishbone Street**

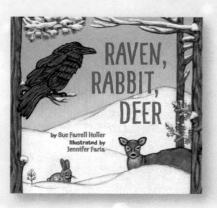

Raven, Rabbit, Deer
Written by Sue Farrell Holler
Illustrated by Jennifer Faria
ISBN: 9781772781366
(hardcover)
32 Pages

"Acrylic and colored pencil artwork...startles with rich winter sunset hues...[A] slow-paced appreciation of the natural world."—**Publishers Weekly ★ Starred Review**

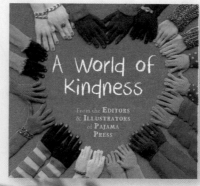

A World of Kindness
Featured art by Tara Anderson
ISBN: 9781772780505 (hardcover) | 9781772781090 (paperback)
32 Pages

"The child-friendly questions posed and the scenarios depicted provide food for thought and discussion about the importance of taking action." —**ILA Literacy Daily**

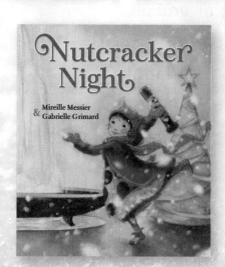

Nutcracker Night
Written by Mireille Messier
Illustrated by Gabrielle Grimard
ISBN: 9781772780918
(hardcover)
40 Pages

"This vibrant tribute to a holiday tradition follows a sensory-filled adventure to a Nutcracker performance....A charming entrée for ballet-bound children."
—**Publishers Weekly**

Let's draw!

Decorate this boy's snowsuit.

Let's solve the puzzle!

Help the **snow plow** clear the road to the school.

Let's draw!

What is the grandfather pointing at?
Draw a **bird** in the sky.

Let's solve the puzzle!

Solve the secret code.

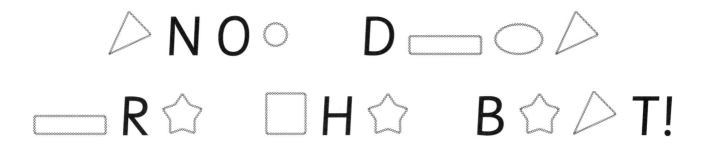

| ⬭ = Y | ▢ = T | ◦ = W |
| ▭ = A | ☆ = E | △ = S |

△ N O ◦ D ▭ ⬭ △

▭ R ☆ ▢ H ☆ B ☆ △ T!

(SNOW DAYS ARE THE BEST!)

Let's draw!

Is this girl dancing in the snow? Is she at a skating rink? You decide! Draw a background for her winter fun.

Let's solve the puzzle!

Which **block** made each print in the snow?

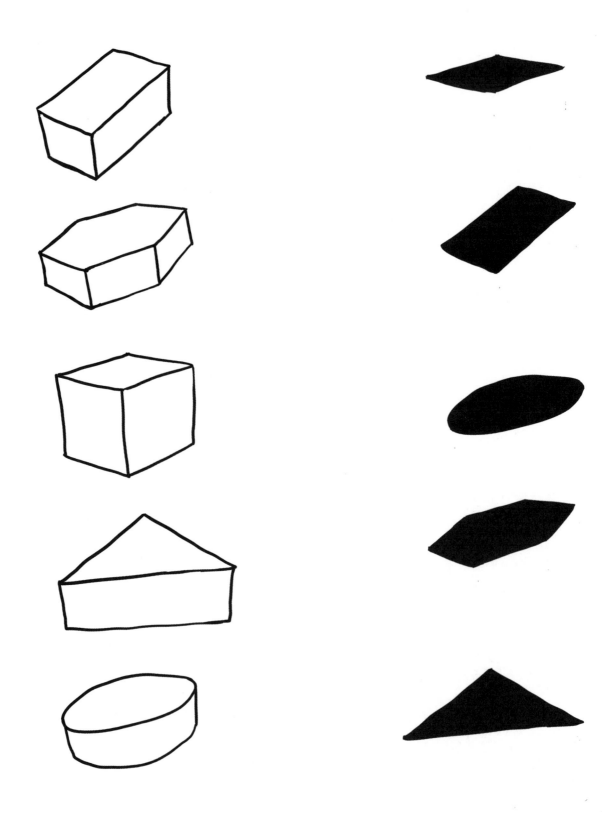

Let's solve the puzzle!

Join the dots.

Let's solve the puzzle!

Choose the rhyming word to complete the poem.

SNOW   ICE   FUN

When puddles freeze
And cold winds blow,
I make a wish
for lots of _____ !

Let's draw!

Design an awesome snow fort!

Let's solve the puzzle!

If every **snowflake** has **six sides**, how many sides are there on...

Two snowflakes?

Three snowflakes?

Four snowflakes?

Let's color!

Let's solve the puzzle!

Circle 5 differences in the pictures

Snowflakes on My Nose

1 2 3 4 5

word search

DEER   FOX   OWL
RAVEN   RABBIT

```
R   A   V   E   N   D
A   C   G   N   F   E
B   P   F   O   X   E
B   P   H   W   E   R
I   I   J   L   K   L
T   J   B   M   E   D
```

Let's draw!

Draw a **snowman** using:

5 circles   1 rectangle   1 semicircle

1 triangle   1 square

Let's match!

Match each snowflake to its shadow.

Let's color!

Use the code to color each section. A secret picture will be revealed!

BLUE - 1   YELLOW - 2   BROWN - 3

BLACK - 4   RED - 5   ORANGE - 6

Let's solve the puzzle!

How many more **deer** are there than **spruce trees**?
Color the correct number.

1 2 3 4 5

Let's solve the puzzle!

Label each piece of winter clothing.

HAT   SCARF   MITTENS
BOOTS   COAT

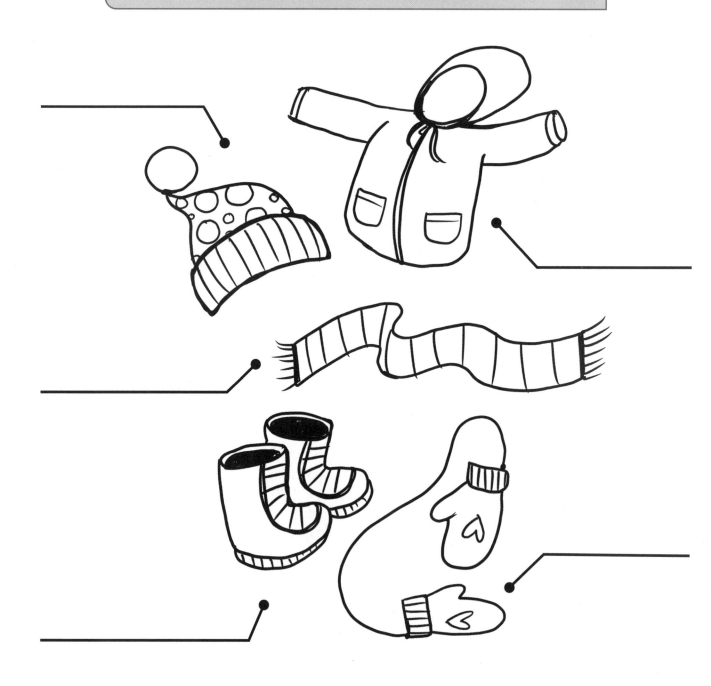

Let's draw!

Dress this child to go outside.

Let's solve the puzzle!

Are these statements true or false?

1. There are fewer than four coats in the picture.   T / F

2. More children are wearing earmuffs than hats   T / F

3. There are at least five buttons in the picture.   T / F

4. The picture shows an equal number of mitten   T / F
   and boots.

Let's solve the puzzle!

What is the **cardinal** saying to her mate?